K]

DENNIS O'DRISCOLL

KIST

THE DOLMEN PRESS

KIST is designed by Liam Miller,
and printed in the Republic of Ireland
for the publishers,
The Dolmen Press, Mountrath, Portlaoise, Ireland.

Publication of this book was assisted by a grant from
An Comhairle Ealaíon (The Arts Council).

First published 1982

British Library Cataloguing in Publication Data:
  O'Driscoll, Dennis
    Kist
    I. Title
    821'.914   PR6065.D/

    ISBN 0 85105 401 3 *Special Edition*
    ISBN 0 85105 396 3 *Pbk*

© 1982: Dennis O'Driscoll

Copyright under the Berne Convention, all rights reserved. Apart from fair dealing for study or review, no part of this publication may be reproduced, stored in a retrieval system, or transmitted, in any form or by any means, electronic, mechanical, photocopying, recording, or otherwise, without the prior permission of the Dolmen Press.

FOR MICHAEL HAMBURGER

ACKNOWLEDGEMENTS

Acknowledgements are due to the following, where some of these poems were first published or broadcast: *Agenda*, *Bananas*, *The Irish Times*, *New Poetry 5* (Arts Council of Great Britain), *Quarto*, *Poetry Australia*, WBEZ Radio (Chicago).

CONTENTS

	Page
Wish	9
Meat	10
Caveat	12
Cancer	15
Thalidomide	17
Flat Life	18
Neighbours	20
Miracles	22
Horology	23
Departures	24
A Christmas Night *after Pasternak*	25
Hops Field *after Pasternak*	26
Village	27
C'mon Everybody	28
War	29
Prayer	30
Kist	31
Post-mortem	32
Elegies	34
Siblings	36
Dissection	37
Contents	38
Theatrics	40
Traces	41
Medical Practitioners	42
Flatland	43
Death Duties	44
Porlock	45
Seasoning	46
Wings	48

Being	49
Someone	55
Dead	56
Breviary	57

WISH

In a children's book, I read how wishbones
could be used as legs for model men.

Then, each taking a leg,
we pulled and broke.

The one who got a leg and groin
also got a wish.

MEAT

I

Like plums
we ripen
on stiff kernel.

Life,
a pressure cooker,
boils us in sweat.

II

A hot kebab
at body heat,
rotting, going off.

Meat on the bone.
No freezer deep enough
to keep it fresh.

III

A double heart transplant:
your heart and mine
beating in time.

Buried in a single body, live,
two lovers
lying in one bed.

IV

I look at books,
anatomy charts.
I kiss you,

muscle, tissue, heart.
Your soft flesh cushions me
from the reality of bone.

CAVEAT

I

navel-knotted balloons
we burst
if cut or weakened
leaving shrivelled skin

our lives carry no guarantee
against structural damage
the human product
is a chance we take

the body is non-durable
its materials not rain- or crushproof
the concrete of its bones
not reinforced

a leg is pruned to increase development
its dead branch cut back
to control the growth rate
of rampant disease

knife whispers through meat
saw screams through bone
with a hollow ring
limb drops in a bucket

and beside freckled arms
defenceless shields of breast
incinerator burns its unused energy
giving solid-fuel heat

II

intimate touch of disease
works through each body
groping with impure fingers
leaving, like weeds, unwanted blossoms
excess varieties of flesh

in the hospital supply shop
tall shelves are weighted with medicines
that promise to remedy the chemical imbalance
we flinch from in student photographs
break arthritic ice, relieve blocked artery drains

annexes are for special requirements
refuse-bag plastic of colostomy
wheelchairs unfolding like stiff wings
man's faltering machine returned
for servicing, repair

at home I test your body like a torturer
trying to find
with fingers warm as a lit cigarette
where your most sensitive parts are
to neutralise with loving

future agony, pain, death

III

slides show a woman
scorched into her fireside chair
her legs both still intact
extend, slippered, from ash

glistening syphilitic sores
a child whose skin
bears marks of his inflammability
rigid attitudes of death...

shaggy-haired human tongues
shock-absorbing hearts
hunched pickled embryos
are stacked in jars on shelves

for the next class we tour wards
through muted antiseptic smells
phlegm, urine samples, meths
it is afternoon

a nurse carries a bedpan
to a drip-fed invalid
a man is shouting prayers
above his pain

visitors mumble behind screens
below us city shoppers
offices and railway tracks
busy in sun

our bleached coats unstained by blood
we try to absorb everything
preparing for our tutor's questions
oral examinations we must face

CANCER

I

the word cancer
brings a lump
to my throat

makes me conscious of the weight
of every body cell
the exhausted air I breathe

II

her skin beaten thin
as gold leaf
bitter lemon

aurora borealis
in a dim hospital ward
smothering my first word

III

with a miner's lamp
the surgeon slices sediments of thought
locates tumours like rare jewels

faceted birth stones
drained from brain's sludge
quarried from an open-cast skull

IV

    this patient attending radiation
    is anchored to an arm
    doctors prime an ocean blue

    a chart of his malignancy
    a tattoo representing death
    a high water mark of pain

V

    dab smears, biopsies
    a new star in the molecular galaxy
    matched with the cytologist's chart

    the penis equipped to discharge seed and urine
    crumpled testicle and fondled breast
    no longer benign organs now

THALIDOMIDE

as if amputated before birth
they too are mindful
of the pain of absent limbs

our own skin-crusted meat pies
contain homogeneous ingredients
intestine sausage, cauliflower brain, kidney and spare rib

this regulation kit is our equipment
standard issue designed to fight for life
though blood will leak, strain and exposure kill

some bodies are fashionable for a season or two
worshipped, promoted, photographed, desired
pliable 'models' of humanity

but these others, hidden away, do not attain
even minimal requirements of quality
'normal' children stare, parents blame themselves

for flippers, club feet, faces paralysed
no ears or anus, genitals deformed
fingers fringing a shoulder, blind split-level eyes

and this is the only existence a child will know
whose hands a neighbour cannot find
to press inside the customary shilling of luck

FLAT LIFE

I

We listen to noises they must make to live:
window-box of television, a perennial bloom,
world now gazes through;
stylus injecting records against silence;
telephone arguments; top-40 shows...

Tonight, even thunder adds percussive sounds,
forked tongues of lightning poison sky.
When, eventually, you sleep
I strain for murmurs from your heart,
the soothing metre of your breath.

But, draining beer tins, tapping denim legs,
tenants still watch detectives shoot
behind bulletproof T.V. glass,
or ears are stereo receivers for rock beat,
dead language of disc-jockeys kills their time.

II

Mornings here are quiet.
Water from spring showers
gargles in dry soil, sprinkles grass.
A grey fur of dust grows over our possessions.
Early swallows skim across an ocean-blue sky,

the few white clouds like foam;
their circling a ripple on its still water.
Silence and water are my natural elements
before speakers deface quiet, scattering its dust.
Your body is still sunk under blankets,

covers rising and falling like a sea
that laps now to your breathing, a great lungfish;
as a shaft of sun filters through the window
blowing the room, like glass, into a globe,
a sudden bubble of frail light.

NEIGHBOURS

I

an organism of sound
begins to throb

I feel its pulse
its beat

II

pause between their records
is our breathing space

until fresh airs begin

III

drums like rattlers amplified
their music screams for notice

as they swig six-pack bottles
suck a soother-cigarette

hell is other people you hiss
when party smoke swelters

through our floorboards
from their underworld

IV

We dream of quiet
broken only by Mozart,
long throat of clarinet
to clear the cobwebbed air.

This evening, I can hear your needles,
crossed like swords,
foaming with white wool,
knitting patient webs of lace.

Outside, as if snow had bleached streets,
a single, slow car drifts,
across the hillside
and into slush of clouds.

MIRACLES

I *Cana*

Making a chalice
of the glass
he wounded water,

keeping his blood,
his good wine,
until last.

II *Desert*

Loaves were multiplied
until the poor, imprisoned even,
would eat bread.

Beneath its crusted dome,
freshly each day,
he chose to come.

III *Calvary*

an icicle
his frozen body drips

our wrongs rust
his forgiving palms

his death a red sunset
brings the next day fair

HOROLOGY

I
ticking inside

on my face
you can read time

II
gold hair is devalued

sun-like dandelions
wear silver then

full moons

III
a standing stone
in a circular ditch
is the oldest sun dial
telling our time in millenia

IV   *Watches*

hands orbit:
a speedometer
measuring our pace

digital:
yours calculates
the miles

V   *Clock*

oily its arms move
exorcising us from rooms

DEPARTURES

I

Grain from the barn of memory.

You were the long churn of a lily,
the spilt milk of love.

II *after Vinokurov*

Objects speak louder than words.

And here is the stone that made the river dance.
Here is the gate that opened to friends once.

III

Glass coffin of an airport has consumed you.

Your jet ploughs sky.
Its wings, like fingers, lift you out of reach.

A CHRISTMAS NIGHT
after Pasternak

A candle, melting faster now,
the year begins to spill wax tears of snow.
They draw to your bright room
like beads of mistletoe.

Snowdrift walls, like hesitations, separate us.
But, as moths hover towards flame,
my longings swarm across the countryside
and beat against your windowpane.

And in a silver-plated darkness then,
I cross iced fields and strain to see
the candle burning welcome in your window,
star-like, drawing me.

HOPS FIELD
after Pasternak

Under the sheets of rain we wait,
where ivy spirals towers of trees:
the coat a bridge across our shoulders,
my hand flowing about your waist.

Nervously, our damp fingers mix,
your hair, plaited as hops, an intoxicant:
and what was shelter, love;
what was coat, a bed.

VILLAGE
For George Mackay Brown

sea lathers a scalp of rock
white fringes of deep waves toss

blackberry thimbles dangle from a needled bush
smoked cod, like varnished planks, hang in a shed

the small football stadium is a deserted amphitheatre
the telephone in its red kiosk rings and rings

hazy mountains are outlined like isotherms
noon airways broadcast peace

no shoppers, fishermen, schoolchildren in sight
no dog stretched under the wave-curling sun

no watercoloured jellyfish like melting ice
no bird flock shimmers on a wash of sky

and a petrified silence settles
like the pause after the whale,

its tail shaped like pleading arms,
is sucked into digestive juices of the sea

in craft shops built of oatmeal stone
kilns are warm still

on the roofless forge a tattered poster blows
its message, 'NO URANIUM', still partly legible

C'MON EVERYBODY

every morning
everybody in the world
begins the day with radio

the television set
is like a leftover meal
an unwashed dish in the cold living room

everybody in the world
is singing the same
number one song

nobody looks outside where clouds
are gathering in a mushroom shape
forecasting bad weather

everybody in the world
dying together
of the radium

WAR

I

somewhere between
backbone sword
bloodbath of the heart
we hide

II

the skull
is not a tin hat

glass in eyes
not bulletproof

III

sky cobbled
with bombers

unlike atoms
man can be created
and destroyed

IV

like salt on snails
fallout liquefies

we burn down
to a wick of bone

marshlight of pale skin
glow worms feed on

PRAYER

Streets flood, thunder erupts,
wind-bent sycamore
is peeled of orange leaves.

Autumn's spreading rust,
our fire glows;
and I imagine refuge:

working together, reap and sow,
chancel chipped by rain,
rustling paper, plainsong,

smoothing snow of prayer.
If I could find a God
then I would believe,

bowing before its wind, its power.
I try to pursue music,
thunder, fire,

until they discover for me
this God
whom, already, I adore.

KIST
i.m. 14th February 1975

On that lovers' morning, our hearts chimed.
Later, the slow death knell of hers
and a coffin door slamming
in her last chill breath.

Preparing me for your death, then,
I noticed silver strands,
coffin-handle bright,
beneath your oak-brown hair.

And, pacing behind hearse,
my own face in its glass
took on the wrinkled grain
of coffin wood.

POST-MORTEM
in memory of my father

I

since the minutes
of our last meeting
I can record

only your departure
for the infinite
and my substantial loss

II

across the red carpet of blood
which you rolled out
to welcome us

and over the bare boards
of your coffin I walk
trying to furnish a home

III

bowls of pipes you enjoyed
are like burnt-out ground now
where you had camped
then left without a trace

like the scorched grass
where I had set fire to your clothes
and watched your soul
drift out in tattered smoke

or like the diaries,
the life,
you made a pyre of
shortly before death

IV

we still relive the isolation of your dying
the wound of your decease will not heal
it continues to weep

I remember anniversaries as I walk along mnemonic streets
or those I travelled through to visit you in hospital
checking a watch against the funeral undertaker's clock

every day since you died
I have diagnosed the cause, prescribed imaginary cures
daily acted doctor, coroner, registrar of death

ELEGIES

I

sapling
that was planted
at his birth

is ready to yield
coffin wood now:
its rings

like ripples spread
to count
his submerged years

II

we are digging
on this spring day
burying an exhausted gardener

his stiffly-folded
cigarette-stained fingers
brown as clay

the weeping cherry
he planted
beginning to bud

III

a snowdrop host
our only solid food
melts in the mouth

we are drunk
on altar wine
a rare blood group

seeking strength to face
the gathering crowds
of dead

IV *Credo*

we thank thee
for the suffering
that never abates

for orphaned children
incurable illness
loneliness, despair

for the proof they bring
that thou art always present
everywhere

V

he is stored
in the gold bullion
of an oak coffin

overhead the earth's scars heal
flowers are dyeing countryside
a road worker is in full song

and only we can tell
that sunlight casts
one shadow less

SIBLINGS

I am writing at exactly the moment
you had sent me the message of his death
precisely this time last year.

Returning home from school to an empty house,
you have begun to live your own lives with the vulnerability
of those who know how thin the barrier of flesh is,

that looking forward becomes looking back
until there is nothing either way but death.
It is quiet in the office as I write,

hiding this paper under a file,
heat rising from radiators, first cigarettes being lit,
someone whistling, someone listing soccer scores.

We have spent a year without him now,
his thoughts scattered, his burden of organs eased.
This is just another working day here

of queries, letters, tea-breaks, forms.
Any minute now some telephone will ring
but I do not dread its news as I did then.

I concentrate upon this moment, cup it in my hands,
to understand what the shedding of his skin might signify
and what you have lost in these past years

in which home has become orphanage
and we have soiled the carpet in the hall
with the clay of their two burials,

our world refracted by a lens of tears.

DISSECTION

We thought we had learned the rudiments of life,
thumbing through swapped magazines:
girls with smoothly-threaded skin,
nipples like valves, inflated tubes of breast;

blushing red tunnels lead to corrugated sheds of womb;
legs open on slit flesh, gleaming with scented juice.
Later, at dissection class, we smelled perfumes of death,
slicing her frozen stare,

a layered pasta of muscle and stale beef;
gristle roots from which clots, hard berries, grew.
We pierced the blue sachet of eye,
cracked cockle skull to remove the slime of brain.

Trying to distract ourselves from death,
we returned that evening to the magazines:
unable to enjoy prime cuts of well-hung meat,
raw centre loins they nakedly displayed.

CONTENTS

I *Blood*

gravy
flowing through man's meat

red jam
that sets only in clots

hot running water
the heart pumps

II *Heart*

a rigged-up plug
its cable arteries
connect us to life

but like a fuse it blows
turning the mind's light out
freezing the body's rooms

III
(*on the day a man
received the heart
of a schoolgirl donor*)

the house is flooded
with unexpected sunshine
we wade through light

it is a day
for short sleeves, sandals
for a change of heart

feeling the throb
of a sixteen year old
schoolgirl's joy

inside us

THEATRICS

the dead donor's spare part is trapped in a cardboard tissue box
and rushed in a getaway car
to where, in another guarded room, the victim lies
gagged and bound with tubes, crossed wires
around him muzzles, balaclavas, veils

then a seam is cut, his cell-perforated chest ripped
until muscle and stuffing glisten
reddening self-consciously beneath lights' stare
the murderers rinse the fresh heart like a potato
salt is rubbed into its wounds

they have blood on their fingers, varnished nails
they are caught red-handed, sticky
the one who has prepared the joint passes it around
until, trimmed, it is ready
for the burning fat-coated oven of the open chest

the worn organ is ejected, swimming in a kidney basin
like raw meat vomited
next the new part is screwed in place
with steel tools, coolant, a shock start
and the damaged canvas of skin will be stitched up

its original pigment slowly, expertly restored

TRACES

I

time sieves us into dust
our residue is gall-stone, bone
flesh offers no protection
elbow and back wear through its fabric

II

beneath the surface of our lives
skin deep is buried death
(like underwear we carry skeletons
folded neatly in our trunks)

III

its name is signed
between lines of forehead
in calligraphy of ribs
shakily on wet cardiograph, last will

IV

the body is a spirit level
balanced by the fluids of the ear

even from padded cells of brain
life eventually escapes

bones like scaffolding mark sites
where flesh walls stood

MEDICAL PRACTITIONERS

You stretch like scented nylon on the bed.
I kiss the smooth blood vessel of your body;
flesh, a soft mattress, covers spring-shaped ribs.
Now we forget our illustrated textbooks,

purple eruptions of pox, deformity, disease,
eyes like rippled ice-cream, fungal face: Hallowe'en ghosts
we try to frighten off with surgical masks.
Examining your anatomy, removing, like a bandage, satin
                                                           underclothes,

I feel hard lumps rising in your breasts;
tense and quickening heartbeat, howls for breath;
then slide, a scalpel stab, into your skin.
After this acupuncture, we recover consciousness.

Each organ has a name again now, potential for infection;
from crinkled bark of brain, insects of memory crawl
and the laboratories of time have no formaldehyde
that will preserve, for future students, your perfect specimen.

FLATLAND

Take-away foods, small late-night stores,
record dealers, posters for Folk Mass.
Coke and Kentucky Fried Chicken make an ideal meal here,
unpacked in a bedsitter and swallowed near a one-bar fire.

Down unlit pram- and bicycle-cluttered corridor, by coinbox
                                                                             telephone,
special-offer leaflets, buff uncollected post,
weekends open optimistically beforehand
like sands of package-holiday brochures.

Falling plaster bares timber ceiling ribs,
like piano keys stripped of their ivory; fireplaces are blocked.
Revolving record wheels, slow music after pubs,
will transport lovers into a seagull-velvet dawn,

into stale cigarette smoke, lingering tastes of beer;
outside, ivy-bearded trees shelter the rubbish bins;
milk-cartons roll, great lice, through long-haired lawns;
the hall door buttoned with bells.

In neat gardens on the next street, wickerwork branches
will be baskets full with fruit yet.
Couples yawn and part. Sunday now,
the heavy hours weigh down the scales of watch

to four-o-clock, sports programmes on the radio,
as evening's cigarette-butt is stubbed out,
leaving an ash-grey sky
which only a working Monday will illuminate.

DEATH DUTIES

So many word-perfect books still left unread;
great symphonies not funnelled yet through ears;
landscapes to enter, their air peppermint-sharp to breathe;
paintings that bathe the eye in pure, remedial light...

Instead, dreaming like frozen water behind glass,
I pass routine, duplicated days working on Death Duties,
expert by now on price of coffin pad, habit, hearse hire,
where my initials stand for "date of death" on files
and "I.R.A." means Inland Revenue Affidavit.

When flavour has boiled away from scented evenings,
late clouds collect like steam, or first sparks of stars
ignite black grate of sky,
I am free to spend my rationed afterlife again,
to hold you in hands I borrow, briefly, from an office clock.

PORLOCK

this is the best poem I have never written
it is composed of all the stunning lines I thought of
but lacked the time or place or paper to jot down

this is a poem of distractions, interruptions, clamouring
                                                            telephones
this is a poem that reveals how incompatible with verse my
                                                                     life is
this is a home for mentally handicapped poems

this is the lost property office of poetry
this is my poem without a hero, conceived but never born
this is a prisoner of consciousness, a victim of intelligence leaks

this is the poem that cannot learn itself by heart
this is the poem that has not found its individual voice
this is the poem that has forgotten its own name

this is my most unmemorable creation
these are my most disposable lines
this is the poem that dispenses with words

SEASONING

I *Spring*

the old tree
no longer coughs
phlegm crowns of leaves

birds with arrow beaks
fly from the wind-curved bows
of its branches still

but no green will shoot
through cartridge-like buds
to scare winter away

II *Summer*

dawn's match-head pink
strikes into burning day
cock's palette chest gleams

spider's thumbprint web
sticks to newly-painted hedge
yachts like shark fins scattered across sea

hum of insects everywhere
golden loaves of straw
fresh honeycombs of hay

III *Autumn*

mist pours
from autumn's open fire

the last of sunlight
thatches sky

soon snow will whitewash
walls of air

IV *Winter*

winter bares
icicle teeth
eats fruit and flower

WINGS

like tumbling masonry pigeons drop from a building
magpies flock for gold to where sunset inscribes a tree

the heron paddles with its skirts rolled up
lapwings at their air base wear a crew cut

thrushes pluck a field's loose threads
kettle swans simmer on electric rings

a team of wild geese rows across the evening cheering
and an exhibitionist bat opens a mackintosh

the hawk plays darts, the swallows hoop-la
the drunken cuckoo hiccups one last time

then night's television screen of stars is switched on
a murder story with the owl's loud screams

BEING
for Julie

I *Conception*
juice of being is squeezed from a ripe body
craving with orgasmic joy for life
its bean sprouts hanging by a thread
to dreams of soccer leagues, investment bonds, mince pies

past chiffon folds of mucus
a spoon of sperm cracks open a moon egg
buries a head in its sand
finds its atmosphere habitable

a fossil brands the womb now
the prehistoric zip of spine, the lizard tail
the hard imprint of bone
frozen in molten fluids

in the opening scene
a couple walked the strand
a child's first cry will be
the sadness they feel after coition

II *Entropy*
from the womb everything appeared beautiful
he swam, a goldfish, in the plastic water bag
peering with big eyes
behind the flimsy curtain,

a swollen bubble he longed to pierce:
but now the dented head
becomes a heavy globe
balanced on tilting axis of spine

his nerves, high-tension wires,
bear messages of fear
it is not enough to be a miracle
of raspberry taste buds and bladder greens

an ambulance siren
divides the city traffic
he has drowned his organs in poison
and rushes, sperm-swift, towards premeditated death

III   *Heart*

amplified in the cardiac unit
the businessman's heart is deafening
as the first bang of creation
its valves flap open on a fibreglass moth's wing

artery walls are daubed in cholesterol and smoke
and heart's pothole is choked in clots
curdled blood begins to slake
its insatiable mouth

and it misses the note of life
broadcasting alarm hoarsely
through the loudhailer of stethoscope
its morse tapping an emergency code:

in the operating theatre
light enters tunnels, ventricles, again
heart smacks its rosy lips
revived by a trickling saliva of blood

IV *Brain*

a fig leaf of skin
hides the shameful serpent of intestines
our parcel of flesh is tied
with nerve ends and veins

over which is coiled
the brain's grey rope
a meaty sandwich spread
a cushioned seat of wisdom

preserved under a cracked ceiling
with the pineal body ("site of the soul")
cloud puffy
dreamy between hemispheres

and sometimes cords are purposely snapped
brain's knotted pâté is sliced
or electric shocks
singe troubling memories

V *Eyes*

the meaning of breasts is mastectomy
the meaning of liver is cancer
the meaning of chest is asthma
the meaning of eyes is blindness

their jewels embellish head's cup
producing like oysters
the cultured pearls,
the clear water, of tears

the pupil is a black hole
where clusters of burning stars were swallowed
others shine still, fuelled with beauty,
casting eyelash rays

the cornea is our window
on the outside world
hooding flesh that relishes flesh
and is reflected in its lover's gaze

VI   *Skeleton*

when tight dress of skin,
a body stocking, is threadbare
and wickerwork of muscle
unwinds from biceps and thigh

like elastic bands, a mummy's covering
our classical interior is revealed
carved bust of skull
marble pillars of bone

and pictures painted in blood fade
from walls of head
knowledge, love and dread are emptied
the meat machine halts production

and salted tide of life ebbs
in which foetus gills thrived
leaving a landscape of calcium rocks
our solid foundation stones

VII *Death*

what will be our certified cause of death
will we expire with the lost memory of arteriosclerosis
dissolving in alcohol, crumbling with pain
basted in our own body fat, shivering with old age

our distilled water polluted by cancer, angina, rash
until we resign work and life and suffering
all family fights over, love consummated, arguments resolved
the patiently accumulated facts forgotten:

the red bouquet of heart we offered partners withers
its petalled rose shrivels, its valves harden into thorns
fresh cream of breasts sours, dream topping of skin acidifies
cherry nipples turn to pips

the clock is a wheel of fortune
each second leads to separate destinies, reprieve or death,
its thin hands are the compass needles that direct us
pilot us from time

VIII *Through the Microscope*

the long flowing tresses of a fallopian tube
the crazy paving of cells
the stained-glass window of hormone crystals
the abstract canvas of a city dweller's lung

the rainfall of erected hair
the stranded dolphin of a nerve
the flaming snout of the pulmonary vein
the gaping volcanoes of the colon

the butter yellow of cholesterol
the stratified rock of cones and rods
the magnified saliva of a gourmet
the decayed tooth of racial superiority

the drained kidney of ambition
the white vocal cords of politics like gleaming fangs
the roots of wit and sarcasm inexplicable
the binding agent of life still unidentified

SOMEONE

someone is dressing up for death today, a change of skirt or tie
eating a last feast of buttered sliced pan, tea
scarcely having noticed the erection that was his last
shaving his face to marble for the icy laying-out
spraying with deodorant her coarse armpit grass
someone today is leaving home on business
saluting, terminally, the neighbours who will join in the cortège
someone is trimming his nails for the last time, a precious
                                                              moment
someone's thighs will not be streaked with elastic in the future
someone is putting out milkbottles for a day that will not come
someone's fresh breath is about to be taken clean away
someone is writing a cheque that will be marked "drawer
                                                                   deceased"
someone is circling posthumous dates on a calendar
someone is listening to an irrelevant weather forecast
someone is making rash promises to friends
someone's coffin is being sanded, laminated, shined
who feels this morning quite as well as ever
someone if asked would find nothing remarkable in today's date
perfume and goodbyes her final will and testament
someone today is seeing the world for the last time
as innocently as he had seen it first

DEAD

dead buttocks
wreaths of memory decay
rotting of lips and lips of genitals
mixing of scented juices and semen into soil
purple thighs bait worms
brush-like hair bristles
rusting of bone hinge
puncture of breast and rupture of womb
curtains of coffin silk stirring in burst stomach's wind
porridge of brain spilling from the head's bowl
rainwater drained arterially through heart
nourishing its tentacles of root

a jelly-covered fruit cocktail of organs
drying of pituita sliming of throat
piston limbs polished (their frill of flesh removed) to steel
greased with sour marrow urine oiled
soiling the ragged funeral clothes

in this substance fed recently on fish potato and peas
the taste of baking dies
the smell of chimney smoke
the firm shaking of a hand where veins
were scribbled like a reminder of life

stiff as a sex organ
carried on shoulders it once bore
end of a body's longing for other's heat
workshop smock of skin

intestines splutter like underground gaspings for breath

BREVIARY

Provincial
in Czech
        Holub means pigeon
        Kafka a jackdaw
birds
        we called nuisance
        wanted to shoot

*

Elegy
he was a brilliant poet
until the metre
ran out

*

Spider
a tiny crab
caught
in fishing net

*

Dusk
blue jeans fade
she slips
into a sequined gown

*

Cottage
whitewashed cottage
is a chalk pipe

where brown turf
like tobacco plug is burned

up the stem of chimney
drifts a fragrant smoke

*

Morning
a goldfish
sun swims from the lake

fishbones
comb the tidy waves

on coffee ponds
cream swans float

*

Snow
earth is plaster cast
a red fox trickles
down the mountain path

*

Boy
his hair is a tousled nest
a ragged egg cosy

his oval face
is patterned with freckles

he looks shyly at me
from the white part of his eye

*

Village
bleak ruin
lit only by a naked bulb
of moon

*

At Market
like the peach
she wears a suede coat

buys cut-glass vase
of pineapple

plucks a grape
from the balloon seller's bunch

*

Newgrange
rain spreads
megalithic circles
at the entrance

by midwinter day
sun's pilot light
will glimmer

in the oven tomb

*

Appetite I
fast and abstinence
Good Friday when their god was dead

at Christmas for his coming
ham and turkey leg

*

Appetite II (Eucharist)
the king is dead
a bloody coup:
we queue for rationed bread

DENNIS O'DRISCOLL

Born in County Tipperary in 1954, Dennis O'Driscoll is well known as a reviewer and critic. He has contributed work to *Agenda*, *The Crane Bag* and *The Sunday Tribune* among others, and his poems have also been widely published in magazines. *Kist* is his first collection of poems. Dennis O'Driscoll is at present living and working in Dublin.